Clicker
training
for dogs

KAREN PRYOR

ACKNOWLEDGEMENTS

The publisher would like to thank the following for their
help with photography: Paddy Driscoll, Maggie Cosford,
Shelly Grey, Sue Munchin and June Gillison.

THE QUESTION OF GENDER

The pronoun 'he' has been used throughout the text – but no
gender bias is intended.

Published by Ringpress Books Ltd,
PO Box 8, Lydney,
Gloucestershire GL15 4YN

Designed by Rob Benson.

First Published April 1999 © Sunshine Books, inc.
This edition published 2002 by Ringpress Books

ISBN 1 86054 282 4

Printed and bound in Italy

0 9 8 7 6 5 4 3 2 1

CONTENTS

INTRODUCTION
A Memo From Karen

Dear Dog Lover,

Welcome to clicker training. Clicker training is not someone's new gimmick or special method. Clicker training is dog trainers' slang for a positive reinforcement training system based on operant conditioning, a set of scientific principles describing the development of behaviour in which the animal "operates" on the environment, instead of the other way around. Operant conditioning goes to the root of how animals learn in the natural world; therefore the principles can be applied in any circumstance. The possibilities for dog training are tremendous.

Clicker trainers are developing ways to use this new technology with police patrol dogs; with service and hearing dogs; with puppies, even before weaning; for competition obedience and agility; in hunting, field trials, and tracking; in the breed show ring; in "good manners" classes for pet owners; and in the home.

ABOUT CLICKER TRAINING

Clicker training does not really depend on the clicker; or on food. Clicker training depends on reinforcers, which may be anything the dog likes (toys, petting, etc.) presented with a correctly-timed signal, in such a way that information is communicated between trainer and pet. We start with food as the reward and the clicker as the signal because these are excellent teaching tools, for both you and your dog. Together, you and the dog will be learning a new way of interacting.

Anything you need your dog to know can be taught by reinforcement training. After the dog has learned to understand what behaviour you want, how to do it, and when to do it, you can replace the click with a word, and the food with a pat; a word and a pat, you always have with you.

Once your dog acquires a clicker-trained behaviour (unless you add new rules), the dog will have that behaviour for a lifetime. When the dog knows several behaviours, you no longer will need to click or to praise each one; you can reinforce once, for a whole

Karen Pryor: Pioneer of the clicker training revolution.
Photo: Michael Nastasi, canisphoto.com

repertoire. Eventually, you'll find that you get out your clicker only to sharpen up a response or to teach the dog something new – or just to have fun with your dog: clicker-training is fun for both of you.

But how do you get started? An experienced clicker trainer could teach you the opening moves in a few minutes; but clicker-training teachers are in short supply, and many of us have to learn on our own. This book is meant to get you going: to give you the skills to develop your first clicker-trained behaviours. When you have personally accomplished even a little clicker training, you will find that other books and videos on clicker training will make more and more sense to you. Many thousands of clicker trainers have begun successfully with the information in this book.

The Resources section of this book will tell you where to look for additional information. Also, as a new clicker trainer you may find that you are becoming a resource, yourself, to other pet owners and dog trainers around you. Enjoy it! This is a creative field, and all of us can make a contribution.

CHAPTER ONE

A DOG AND A DOLPHIN

Training without punishment

If you have seen trained dolphin shows at oceanariums or on TV, you will know that dolphins appear to be wonderfully trainable. On command they exhibit all kinds of precision behaviour, including splendid acrobatics and interactive behaviour with other dolphins or with human swimmers. The audience marvels at how eagerly they respond, and how intelligent they must be; wouldn't it be nice if dogs responded like that?

As we dolphin trainers know well, the truth is that dolphins aren't geniuses, and neither are dolphin trainers. The dolphins' speed, precision, and obvious enjoyment of their work is due entirely to the principles dolphin trainers use in training them. And the same techniques can be used on dogs.

OMITTING PUNISHMENT

The first thing to understand about dolphin training is that we are working with animals you cannot punish. No matter how mad you get – even if the animal makes you mad on purpose, by splashing you from head to foot – you can't retaliate. You can't use a leash or a whip or even your fist on an animal that just swims away. You can't starve a dolphin into being co-operative. Dolphins get their fresh water from the fish they eat; if you take away the fish, they rapidly become dehydrated, they lose their appetites altogether, and then they die. Finally, you can't even yell at a dolphin, because they don't care.

Maybe you're thinking "I bet I could think up a way to punish a dolphin...." and I bet you could; but it doesn't matter, because dolphin trainers don't need it.

A dog trained with a clicker is eager and responsive – he loves being given things to do.

Trainers can get whatever they want from a dolphin, using positive reinforcers only: mostly just a chirp or two from a training whistle, and a bucket of fish. We "shape" every behaviour by positive reinforcement. We use positive reinforcement to elicit prompt and correct response to commands – to achieve obedience. We can even use positive reinforcement to discipline an animal – to control misbehaviour such as attacking a tank-mate or refusing to go through a gate (see page 22 for further advice). This sophisticated use of positive reinforcement results in an animal that works brilliantly and loves to work.

The methods we use to train dogs often include the use of force, both to put the dog through required movements and to correct the dog when he makes mistakes, which he inevitably does. Although we may also use praise and petting, unavoidably the dog experiences some confusion, fear, and maybe even physical pain in the training process. Some dogs tolerate these negative experiences well, but dolphins, being wild animals, would not. If you were to train a dolphin by these techniques, the dolphin might learn, but it would offer a sluggish, sulky, unreliable performance; and it might well begin to exhibit aggression toward people. (Does that sound like any dogs you know?)

On the other hand, if you train a dog the way we train dolphins – through positive reinforcement – the dog behaves just like a dolphin: he becomes eager, attentive, precise, co-operative, and capable of a fantastic performance. Here's how it's done.

THE MAGIC SIGNAL

When I talk to dog trainers, a big misconception I run into is that positive reinforcement just means "food." Wrong. The crucial element in getting wonderful behaviour out of a dolphin is not the food reward. The dolphin is not working for the fish; the dolphin is working for the whistle. The sound of the whistle is the magic signal that brings about that wonderful performance.

The first step in training a dolphin is to teach it that every time it hears a whistle, it's going to get a fish. Once the animal knows that the whistle means "Fish is coming" the trainer can use the whistle to mark a behaviour she likes, and then, gradually, to shape or develop something more complex, such as a response to a cue.

For example: suppose, on several occasions, the dolphin heard the whistle (and later got a fish) when it happened to be jumping in the air. Soon it would start jumping every time the trainer showed up. Then it might be allowed to discover that jumping only 'works' when the trainer's arm is raised. So a raised arm becomes the green light, as it were, for jumping.

The trainer could gradually impose other conditions – jumping only 'works' when the direction of the jump is away from the trainer and toward the audience; when the jump is higher than four feet; when the jump occurs within three seconds after the arm is raised. At the end of a few training sessions, the trainer has trained the dolphin to 'take a bow,' on command and with precision. The dolphin has trained the trainer too: "All I have to do is make a certain kind of jump when she sticks her hand up, and she immediately gives me a whistle and a fish every time!"

Note that the whistle is not used as a command. It does not tell the dolphin to start doing something – the hand signal does that. The whistle tells the dolphin, during or at the end of a behaviour, that the trainer likes that behaviour and the dolphin deserves a fish for it. (You don't have to stick with food, either; you can also associate a conditioned reinforcer with a pat, or a toy, or maybe just another chance to work.)

The whistle has now become a conditioned reinforcer.

In the language of psychologists: food, petting, or any other pleasure is an unconditioned reinforcer – something the animal would want, even without training. The whistle, a conditioned reinforcer, is something the animal has learned to want. (Some people use the term 'primary reinforcer' for food and 'secondary reinforcer' for the signal. I avoid those terms because I find it leads people to think that if the whistle is 'secondary' – it should occur after the food – which, of course, makes it meaningless to the animal and useless as a training tool.)

CRUCIAL ROLE

What would happen if you tried to train a dolphin to do a simple jump, away from you, on cue – without the whistle? First, you could not possibly time the fish to arrive when the animal was in mid-jump. So, no matter what kind of jump the animal gave, it would either get the fish later, or get no fish at all. It would have no way of telling why you rewarded one jump over another, or what you liked about the jump. Was it the height? Or maybe the way the animal took off or landed? To develop a jump of a particular height, timing, and direction, you would have to eliminate mistakes by trial and error over many, many repetitions. You would be lucky if the animal didn't get bored (and the trainer too!) before the performance was correct and reliable.

Because of this lack of information, the trainer who uses food rewards without using a conditioned reinforcer typically produces an animal that works eagerly, but learns slowly. We see this in dogs that have

Training with treats is always effective, but without the use of a conditioned reinforcer, i.e. the clicker, a dog may become obsessed by looking for food.

been rewarded with lots of treats without any clear signal as to exactly what behaviour earned the treat. They often seem to be enthusiastic and friendly, but they don't know anything.

Also, when a trainer uses food without a conditioned reinforcer, the animal is apt to look toward the trainer for food all the time. Horses nose your pockets and dogs lick your hands. Dolphins hang around the training station and worship the fish bucket. And with the animal constantly looking at the trainer, it would be difficult to train our dolphin to jump facing away from the trainer, toward the audience.

Once you have established the conditioned reinforcer, however, you can use the whistle to identify behaviour that occurs at a distance, or with the animal facing away from you, with no trouble at all. And the well-conditioned animal, instead of nosing around for a snack, is going on about his business, but also attentively listening for the magic sound, whatever else he may be doing: in horses and dogs that attentiveness is a valuable training asset in itself.

Because of the split-second timing that the marker signal makes possible, the whistle also communicates just exactly what it is that the trainer is looking for. This allows you to teach the animal what you want, in a very clear way, one detail at a time. For example, let's say that a dolphin has assimilated one rule ("Jump facing this way"), and you know that because the animal almost always jumps with the proper orientation when you signal it to jump. Now you can add another detail or rule. You decide "I'll only reinforce the higher jumps." Pretty soon the dolphin has learned one more detail ("I have to jump facing this way, and jump this high").

This step-by-step process may seem elaborate but, in practice, it is a fantastic short-cut to complex, trained behaviour. Even with a naive dolphin, a trainer can develop an on-cue, spectacular, and very specific behaviour (such as the bow I have described), in two or three days – sometimes, if things go well, in a single ten-minute training session. Many times in my dolphin-training experience I have "captured" a behaviour, shaped it into something special, and put it on cue in a single training session; and so have other dolphin trainers.

HOW ABOUT DOGS?

You can easily experience dolphin-training your own dog, using a conditioned reinforcer, in one quick ten-

As soon as you see the dog startle, and look for the treat, you know the signal – the click – has become a conditioned reinforcer.

minute experiment. Some dogs are afraid of whistles. A handy conditioned reinforcer for dogs is a clicker, a small box that goes click-click when you pinch it. They are available in many pet stores, and from websites (see pages 111).

Get yourself a clicker and a few treats. Make the treats small enough so that you can give the dog fifteen or twenty treats without him filling up. Some dogs will work for dry food, especially just before dinnertime, but generally it is better to go for something more tempting.

Teach the dog the meaning of the click by clicking the clicker and giving a treat, four or five times, in different parts of the room or yard (so the dog doesn't get any funny ideas that this only works in one place).

Then click the clicker and delay the treat a few seconds. If you see the dog startle and actively look for the treat, you will know the signal has become a conditioned reinforcer. Now you can establish a behaviour – we call this "shaping."

SHAPING A BEHAVIOUR

An easy behaviour to shape is "Chase your tail." There are, of course, as many ways to elicit this behaviour as there are trainers to think them up: you could turn the dog around by his collar; you could put bacon grease on his tail tip so the dog circles to lick his tail. Here's one way to shape the behaviour "from scratch," without any prompting.

Stop clicking and just wait. Your dog may be intrigued and excited by now; when you do nothing, the dog is likely to move around, and maybe even to whine and bark. The instant the dog happens to move or turn to the right, click your clicker. Give the treat.

Wait again. Ignore everything the dog does, except moving to the right (don't hold out for miracles; one turn of the head or one sideways step with the right front paw is all you need.) If you "catch" the behaviour – if your timing is good – in three or four reinforcements you will see your dog turning to the right further and more often.

Now you will find you don't need to reinforce just a single step to the right, but you can reinforce right turns that go several steps, perhaps through a quarter of a circle; and from a quarter turn, a full circle may come very quickly.

SHAPING A BEHAVIOUR

Griff, a crossbreed, is being taught to turn in a circle. He is clicked for every correct move he makes.

That's a good time to stop the first session: quit while you're ahead, is the golden rule. Put the clicker away, with lots of hugs and praise, and try again the next day, starting with a single step, then a quarter circle, and then more; it will come much faster the second time.

From one circle, the next step is to get two circles, and the next step – an important one – is to go for a variety, rewarding half a circle sometimes, then two circles, or one, or three full turns, or just one and a quarter; this keeps the dog guessing. Once the dog has understood what is required, you can introduce a handsignal or a verbal cue, so that the dog offers his 'trick' only when it is asked for.

This is a silly trick, of course, and not very dignified. There are other behaviours you could use for practice, such as targeting, in which you shape the animal to touch some object with his nose. (Sea lion trainers teach their animals to "target" on the trainer's closed fist; then, by holding their fist on the ground, or in the air, or over a stand, they can move the sea lion where they want, without using force.) The purpose of this experiment is not to teach the dog the trick, but to show you how to use a conditioned reinforcer to shape behaviour, and how effective this kind of reinforcement can be.

WHY USE A CLICKER?

Why do you need to use a clicker? Why couldn't you just use your voice, and the words "Good boy," as the conditioned reinforcer? The main reason is that you can't say a word, even "Good boy" with the split-second precision that you can achieve with a click. With the clicker, and a little practice, you can reinforce very tiny movements – one paw stepping to the right – in the instant that it occurs. A praise word is inevitably rather 'fuzzy,' because it takes longer. The click is also information for you. It teaches you good timing, because you can tell if you clicked too soon or too late – a distinction that is much harder to make if you are using a spoken word.

The second difficulty with using a word is that we also talk near our dogs, and even to our dogs, when we are not reinforcing them. It is hard for the dog to sort the meaningful words out from the stream of noise we make. But the clicker is unlike any other sound in the room, and its meaning is crystal clear. You will, in fact, see the difference very clearly in the way the conditioned dog responds to the clicker (electric attention, galvanised, thrilled) as compared to the way the dog responds to "Good dog!" (What? Oh – smile, wag.)

THE REAL WORLD

Well, I have heard dog trainers say that the clicker is good for tricks but not for anything else – you can't, for example, use it in the obedience ring. Of course not, and you don't need to. The clicker's value is in shaping new behaviour, or refining details; it is not necessary in exhibiting behaviour the animal has already learned. But even in the accomplished champion working dog, the conditioned reinforcer can be a useful training tool. One competitor told me he taught his Dobermann to understand the clicker, and then used it to reinforce her for looking into his face, instead of away from him, while she worked.

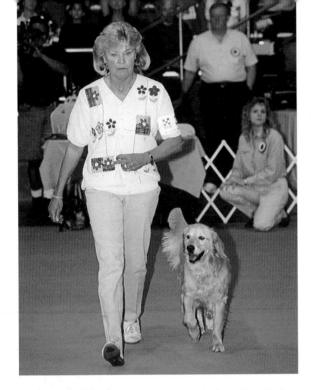

Once a behaviour has been established, there is no need to continually reinforce it.

"It's as if she were grateful for the information, really: it cleared up the vagueness for her," he said. Of course, once the dog had come to understand what was wanted, she did it correctly in the ring, without any clicks.

Don't think, however, that people never use a conditioned reinforcer in the ring. All the trainer has to do is establish a signal the dog is aware of, that no one else notices. I know a keen obedience trainer who uses a barely audible sniff as a conditioned reinforcer. I have seen a competitor convey "Great job!" (as evinced by the overjoyed expression on the dog's face) just by touching one finger to her dog's head. One competitor I know has taught her dog, Rex, that treats are called 'Billy.' Then, as the dog performs in the obedience ring, she can reinforce an especially good behaviour – a nice recall perhaps – with what appears to be a command: "Billy, heel!" No one questions why she doesn't use the dog's usual name in the ring.

◀ *Food, food, food! The dog is enjoying himself, but the overall picture is spoiled.*

How much better it looks ▶ *when the dog is clicked for holding a pose, knowing he will be rewarded later.*

Once a behaviour is learned, using a conditioned reinforcer allows you not only to delay the food, without loss to the performance, but to give less food overall. You don't have to worry that your animal will fill up before the job is done. One example: at dog shows I have often noticed handlers repeatedly baiting or feeding a dog to get a nice pose or an alert expression. Whenever I see that food-food-food going down the dog's throat, I know at once that the person doesn't understand conditioned reinforcers! How much more effective it would be to shape the pose, to develop a verbal cue, and then to reinforce the dog with a click for assuming and holding the proper posture for a respectable length of time. The food reward would follow later, outside the ring, or when the judge has moved on.

The virtue of the conditioned reinforcer is that it works – it conveys information, and affects the animal's behaviour – in all kinds of situations in which real reinforcement is not merely undesirable, but, in fact, impossible. Think, for example, of how useful a simple conditioned reinforcer would be in training scent discriminations, tracking, long sits and downs, go-outs, pointing and flushing birds, and all other dog behaviours that require the animal to work away from you.

CONTROLLING BAD BEHAVIOUR

It might seem unreasonable that you can control bad behaviour with positive reinforcement instead of "correction," but dolphin trainers have many ways to do it. Here are three examples:

1. Establish A Conditioned Negative Reinforcer

This does not need to be a signal that means "I'm going to beat you", but a signal that means "Nope, I'm not going to reinforce you." It tells the animal that some particular effort he is making is not going to pay off. For example, you could simply turn your back on the dog. The animal swiftly learns that whenever he gets this "red light" or "wrong" signal, he should change what he is doing. You could use such a signal, for example, to help teach a dog not to jump up, in greeting, but to keep his paws on the floor for a patting reinforcer.

If your dog misbehaves, such as jumping up, you need to make it clear that you will not reinforce this type of behaviour.

However, when he has four feet on the ground, he is rewarded.

2. Use Positive Reinforcement To Train An Incompatible Behaviour

In our dolphin shows at Sea Life Park, one animal took to harassing the girl swimmer who performed in the show. Rather than give the swimmer a stun gun (or some such punishment), we trained the dolphin to push on an underwater lever for a whistle and fish, and we asked the animal to do that when the swimmer was in the water. The dolphin could not press his lever and pester the swimmer at the same time; the behaviours are incompatible (and apparently lever-pressing was more reinforcing, because the swimmer harassment ceased). You are using this technique if you teach your dogs to lie in the living room doorway, at mealtimes, so they can't beg at the table.

3. The Time-out

Sometimes a dolphin does something really bad, such as showing aggression (swinging its head or teeth at the trainer's hand, for example). The instant this happens, you turn your back, snatch up your training props and fish bucket, and leave, for one full minute. That's the end of all the fun. The dolphin is apt to stick his head out of the water looking dismayed – "Hey, what did I do?" In a few repetitions, he learns to mind his manners. The doggy equivalent would be the same: put the treats and clicker away, and end the fun.

Time-outs are used successfully by oceanarium trainers to eliminate aggression toward human swimmers, even in highly dominant animals such as adult male killer whales. The technique is, however, distressing to the animals and must be used sparingly.

MENTAL ATTITUDES

Using reinforcement is a lot of work for the trainer, because it forces you to think. Oh no, what pain! It's so much easier just to follow someone else's rules: If the dog makes a mess, rub his nose in it; if the dog doesn't heel, jerk the chain. However, in thinking out what you are going to reinforce, you will be a better trainer. And the focus you will need, in order to perfect the timing of your reinforcers, makes training a thrill instead of a bore.

From the animal's standpoint, this kind of training is not a matter of learning how to stay out of trouble by doing what's required – a chore and nothing more. Instead, this kind of training gives the animal a chance

REAPING REWARDS

Clicker training gives your dog a chance to win, again and again. Here, Mich, a Rottweiler crossbreed, is being trained to balance a treat on her nose ready to catch it.

Click! Mich is rewarded for offering the correct behaviour – and she gets the treat.

to win, over and over again, and also a chance to control at least part of his world. For example, from a dolphin's standpoint, once he has learned the meaning of the whistle, the training is not an exchange of commands and obedience, but a guessing game in which the dolphin tries to "discover" various ways to make the trainer blow that whistle. It is a game, with strict rules, but with equality on both sides. No wonder the dolphins enjoy their obedient trainers!

The effect of using the conditioned positive reinforcer is, in fact, far more powerful than merely giving free goodies could ever be. If you stop relying on control of misbehaviour, and start shaping good behaviour with clear-cut conditioned signals for reinforcement, your dog will respect you in a new way. To your dog, you will be making sense, at last.

CHAPTER TWO

GETTING STARTED

A few easy behaviours
to train with a clicker

We usually think of a well-trained dog as one that doesn't do anything wrong: doesn't jump up at visitors, doesn't bark too much, doesn't get on the couch, and so on. We usually think of "training," therefore, as a matter of getting rid of bad behaviour. Training is what we do to stop the dog from jumping up, barking, and pulling on the leash. So, conventional training often seems to consist largely of control and prevention. You push on your dog or yank on his leash to make him do something, and then correct him, usually with another yank on the leash, when the dog does it "wrong," until he learns how to do it "right."

Clicker training provides a new way of learning.

Clicker training, or operant conditioning, is quite different. Clicker training can produce a well-behaved dog, but by a new path. Instead of stopping the dog from doing the wrong things, we are going to teach him to do the right things. He will learn to greet visitors politely, to bark at the right time, to walk on a loose leash, to go only where dogs are supposed to go (on the floor, not the couch, on the lawn, not the flowerbeds) and so on.

Some people approach dog trainers as if they were going to a doctor, or a garage mechanic. "Here's my problem. Tell me what's wrong and how to fix it." Clicker trainers don't work that way. Our aim is to give you the tools for building behaviour in general. When you understand the system, you can build any behaviour you want.

There are no set recipes for developing specific behaviour with the clicker and treats. I might train a specific behaviour, such as walking politely on a loose leash, one way, and clicker author Morgan Spector, might train it another; other clicker trainers might have good and workable ways of their own. What follows is a simple guide to a few basic behaviours, not to be followed religiously, but to give you a place to start. You can begin with any of these behaviours; your dog may find one kind of task easier than another at first. You can work on all of them, even in a single session, if you want. Experiment!

If you run into problems, look first at the "Clicker Tips" (page 75), and "Frequently Asked Questions" (page 85). It's probable that other people have experienced the same problems, or asked the same questions, when starting out. Use the resources available. You can teach yourself this art, by trial and error, and study. Many people have done so already.

Remember, too, that each training session with each dog is different. You have to "wing it" and use your imagination. Sometimes pets catch on faster than people! Be patient with yourself, and have fun.

THE BASICS

Operant conditioning is an active, participatory experience, like dancing, or making music. You won't learn how to do it by reading about it, or by arguing, about it. You need to try it. For that you need a pet, something the pet likes to eat, and two or three minutes of spare time.

To get ready for a clicker-training session, prepare twenty or thirty cut-up treats. Make the pieces small: I suggest pea-size. If you have a Maltese Terrier, one piece is big news. If you have an adult Great Dane, give several pea-sized bits at once, so the dog knows there is something in his mouth.

If the treat is too large, or takes too long to chew, you will find problems before you have even got started. Clicker training is all about *timing*, and that includes the rhythm of the shaping interchange, which is part of the learning. If the rhythm is constantly interrupted (by, for example, irregular pauses for chewing) both the dog *and you,* will soon feel like doing something else. "Let's see what's on TV" (you); "Let's see if any other dogs were in my area last night" (the dog). So: make sure, at least at first, that your pay-off is delicious and easy to eat; then both of you can get on with the communication.

THE FIRST SESSION

Your first session may be only a few minutes long, but you need peace and quiet in those minutes. After all, you (not just the dog) are learning something new. You need to be free of meaningless interruptions.

Pick a place where there are no distractions and where you both feel at ease. The living room is fine, or the kitchen. (Outdoors there are too many other things for the dog to think about.) Wait until you and the dog can be alone; the *last* thing you need is onlookers telling you you're doing it wrong. If you have other pets, put them elsewhere temporarily.

Put the treats in a dish or bowl where you can reach them, but where the dog cannot. Be prepared to move around while you are training; don't always just sit on the couch. If you are moving, your dog will find it easier to get moving, too.

Some dogs are not very interested in food treats at first. That's fine; once they catch on to the meaning of

When you introduce the clicker, choose a place that is free from distractions.

the clicker, a zest for treats will develop naturally. It is always a good idea to have your first brief click sessions right before the dog's usual mealtime. Then the dog's normal appetite is working in your favour, to help you gain the dog's interest and participation.

HOW ABOUT PUPPIES?

You can start clicker training a new puppy the day you get him home. There is nothing frightening or potentially harmful in clicker training, so you don't have to wait until your puppy reaches some specific age to begin. Furthermore puppies, being little food-seeking missiles, *love* finding out how to make you click, and often learn faster than older dogs.

Clicker training works for all dogs, regardless of age, breed or experience.

You can, of course, start clicker training with a dog six months old, or six years old, or sixteen years old. They can all enjoy this game. Also, it doesn't matter what breed of dog you have, or what sex, or what temperament: clicker-training is fine for hyper enthusiastic bouncing-off-the-walls dogs, and for quiet, dignified, or timid souls too.

Here are several different starting exercises for you and your dog to practise on: "Sit and down," "Come when called," "Walk on a loose leash," "Target training," and "101 things to do with a box." You may begin with any one. You may try all of them. Some dogs take to one behaviour more easily than another. If, after three or four short sessions, you don't seem to be making progress, feel free to shift to a new behaviour, and then come back to the old one later on.

THE SIT AND DOWN

To begin: Get your treats ready. Click and simultaneously hold out a treat right under your dog's muzzle, so he can get it easily. Move a little: repeat this several times. These few first clicks and treats are just to help the dog understand what the click means. Vary the length of time between the click and the arrival of the treat: sometimes immediately, sometimes a beat or two later. Always give the click first, and then the treat. Keep your treat hand quiet, or behind your back, until you click, so you don't inadvertently give the dog false cues by unconscious hand movements. Sometimes you might want to wait a few seconds after you give the treat, before you click again, to help the dog become more aware of the importance of the click.

Now click and toss a treat to the floor (or on to a plate) where the dog can see it. Help the dog find the treat if necessary. You are showing the dog that the click always means food is coming, *but* it may not come in the same place every time, and it may not come right away. Do this two or three times.

Some clicker trainers like to condition the dog to the clicker by repeating this introductory process many, many times. I prefer just to get on with it. As soon as the dog is pricking his ears when he hears the click, I think it's time to give the dog (or any animal) the most important information of all: that his own actions can cause the click to happen.

 STEP ONE

To start: hold the clicker in your dominant hand, the treats in the other. Holding the treat in your closed hand, move your hand backwards over the dog's head, between his ears, so he looks up. Click the upward look. Repeat. Back up a step or two, coax the dog towards you, and click him if he looks up at your face. Repeat.

Now lean over the dog, just a little. This should make the dog lean backwards so his tail end lowers. Click that movement. Treat. Repeat. Work fast and click often; it's better to give a click for nothing much (eye contact, say) rather than let time go by with no rewards so the dog loses interest. Watch the hind legs; when they start to fold, click.

CLICKER TRAINING THE SIT

① *Misty, a Border Collie puppy, has already been introduced to the clicker. She is now being taught to sit. The treat is held above her head. As she looks up, she will lower her tail-end towards the ground.*

② *Click! Misty is clicked as soon as she offers a Sit.*

③ *It does not matter if the pup gets up when the food reward is given. It is the click that marks the correct behaviour.*

At some point, the dog will sit. Click and give the treat immediately. Back up a step, coax the dog to you, wait, and see if the dog will sit without any hints from you. Click. Repeat. Move sideways a step or two. Smile at the dog, catch his eye, and pause – the dog will usually do his 'lucky sit' again. Click and treat!

When you click, and make the treat available, the dog will usually jump up again. That's *fine*! Contrary to conventional training, we don't care what the dog is doing when we feed him: only when we click. Your click "marks" the behaviour you want. The dog will remember what he was doing when you clicked, without any help from you.

By the way, if the dog doesn't sit at first, be patient. Use your closed hand and the treat to try luring the dog's head backwards again. Don't push the dog. Don't tell him what to do. ("Don't tell him what to do?! How will he know what to do?!") Don't worry. In clicker training, we don't start by ordering the dog around. First, we get the behaviour. Later, we'll name the behaviour.

What if the dog jumps all over you? Ignore that behaviour. Wait for it to die down. When the dog puts his front feet back on the ground, start the hand movement again.

 STEP TWO

Now we're going to increase the length of time the dog will sit. Wait until he sits. Click. Treat. The next time the dog sits, don't click right away. Move your treat hand away. Click. Treat.

By delaying the click a little, you are teaching the dog to sit there and stay there until he hears the click. You do not need to keep clicking to encourage the dog. For now, the click ends the behaviour. By withholding the click, you can extend the duration of the behaviour. Don't talk to the dog or gush over him; that will just add confusing non-information. Be quiet.

ENDING THE SESSION

Research has indicated that many short training sessions are much more effective than a few long ones. Your first sessions might be no longer than four or five minutes. Quit while you and the dog are still having fun. You may get no further than Step One or Step Two in the first lesson, or even the first two or three lessons. That's fine. On the other hand, you may find yourself with one of those whirlwinds that wants to play this new game for half an hour or more, or one that goes all the way through to Step Six in the first lesson. That's fine, too. Some dogs might give you Step Three or Four before you have accomplished Step Two. That's fine; go ahead with the step you have got, and go back to the earlier step later. (If you only got in two clicks for some desirable behaviour, that's fine! Each click counts.) The important thing is to make progress, however small.

If the dog quits on you (as they may, at first, when they are just learning this game) or if *you* get confused or feel yourself getting impatient or angry, stop at once and try again later. You will find that an amazing amount of learning goes on between training sessions, especially if you keep them short. You may find that a problem that eludes you today will straighten itself out tomorrow.

 ## STEP THREE

When the dog is initiating the "sit" on his own, and when he can sit for a few seconds without your hand in place, you can start using your treat hand in a new way: to tempt the dog into lying down. Put your treat hand (fist closed, treat inside) to the dog's nose, as he is sitting. Then move it down, slowly, between the dog's front paws, very close to the dog. The nose will follow the hand, the dog is likely to lean backwards, and then to start to lie down. Click when the front legs start to buckle, the first time. Treat. The second time, lure him a little farther down, pulling your hand away gently when he touches the floor. Does the dog lie down? Good. Click. Does the dog pop up, then? Fine. Doesn't matter. Give him the treat while he is standing. Then lure him down again.

 ## STEP FOUR

At some point – and this is your judgement call – gently reduce your luring motion downward. Let the dog know you have food, but don't lead his nose down. Wait. You are waiting for the dog to try lying down, *on his own*.

You don't need to wait for the complete "lying down" behaviour. Click if one paw just starts to slide out, or his front elbows start to bend; or even if the dog dips his

CLICKER TRAINING
THE DOWN

Now Misty is sitting reliably, the treat can be used to lure her towards the ground.

As soon as she goes into the Down, click and reward.

The lure can gradually be withdrawn, and Misty is clicked for staying in the Down position.

head toward the floor. Your click (followed by a treat) communicates to the dog that he is thinking along the right lines: going floorwards. Wait again; give him time. This time, let him go a bit further. Maybe all the way down.

Repeat. Watch the dog. You may actually see, on the dog's face, the moment when "the lightbulb goes on" – the moment when he realises that if he lies down, you will click! Even tiny puppies, six or eight weeks old, can figure this out. That's when your pup will begin to lie down on purpose. The dog may even fling himself to the floor. If that happens, you can signal your pleasure not by clicking repeatedly – always give one click only – but by giving him a whole handful of treats: a dramatic event we call a jackpot.

As trainer Lana Mitchell puts it, for you this is a training game; but it's a thinking game for the dog. When your dog realises, consciously, that by lying down and waiting, he can make you click – when the dog discovers he can *earn* his own treats – he has learned something wonderful that we can build on in many, many ways. It is an important first lesson; and an exciting one for the dog.

TRAINING NOTE

It's always a good idea to start each session by going back a step. If you got to Step Five, and the dog was lying down on his own, begin the next session with a quick review of Step Four, luring the dog into a down, then waiting and clicking for a partial down, then for a full down on his own. Two or three "review" clicks will usually bring the dog up to speed so you can go on.

The next steps for any behaviour, including "Down", are to extend the duration of the behaviour, to add distractions, and to attach a cue: a hand signal, or a word, or both. To proceed with these steps, turn to page 67: "Increasing your Clicker Training Skills."

"COME WHEN CALLED"

Coming when called! The bugbear of all pet owners. Training a reliable "Come" is simple, but it's not easy. It takes thought, attention, and some common sense. The clicker will be a great help.

 ## STEP ONE

Sit on the floor. Coax the dog over to you. When he gets to you, click and treat. Get up. Move. Try again. Repeat.

Call the dog when he is in another room. Click and treat when he gets to you. Do this at odd times of the day and when unexpected. *Always* click and treat when the dog responds. If the dog does not respond, don't give him a second chance. Let him see you put the clicker and treats away (or, even better, let the dog see you click and treat another dog, or the cat.)

Children can help. Position the children on both sides of the room and have them do this: One child calls the dog's name. When the dog looks, the child says "Come," and pats the floor or whatever is necessary to get the dog to come. (Don't wave treats! Hide the treats.) Click when the dog arrives. Then the child gives a little treat and the other child calls the dog.

Even a puppy soon thinks this is a great game, romping back and forth between two kids with clickers and treats.

 STEP TWO

Try it outdoors. If the dog is a real bolter, use three people. One holds the dog on a long leash, and the other two call the dog back and forth between them. Remember that the important element for developing reliability is not the food, not the call, but the click when the dog gets to the person. That is when the learning occurs.

Take the dog for walks. An extending, flexible leash, which winds itself up into a little box, is nice, because it allows the dog to get quite far away from you, feeling quite free, without actually being free. Every now and then, call the dog, from near or from far, and click and treat when he comes to you. If he ignores you, walk on another ten or twenty paces and try again.

If the dog pulls constantly, shorten the leash, stand still, and let the dog pull until he gives up. Then call him, even if he is right next to you; when the head turns, click, and treat. Don't yank the dog, or scold him for not coming; that just teaches him that "Come" means "trouble."

Every time you call your dog, and he comes, be sure to click. If you have no clicker with you, use a tongue click, or the word "Good" (not as clear, but better than

CLICKER TRAINING COME WHEN CALLED

Misty is working on the "Come" command in the park. The training line is being used as insurance so that she doesn't run away. It is not used to pull her, or to reel her into position. To begin with, Misty is clicked and rewarded for being held by the collar.

The first handler stays with Misty, while the second handler goes a short distance away. As soon as the second handler calls her name, Misty is released.

Misty heads for the second handler.

The moment she reaches the second handler, Misty is clicked and given a treat.

nothing.) Don't let the dog run around loose in public places until you have an enthusiastic return to you well established. This may take weeks, especially if the dog has been ignoring "Come" for years. With a new puppy, it might not take more than a few days.

STEP THREE: GOING FREE, OUTDOORS

When you do let your dog loose, away from home, do it, at first, in a fenced place, and preferably a really boring place. Let the dog have a good sniff around, and then use your "Come" and make it stronger by going down on your knees invitingly. Click, jackpot, and go home. Make that first, one-trial lesson memorable.

If you are outdoors, and the dog doesn't come, go and get the dog. Put the leash on, and take the dog home or inside. Don't give him four or five chances to ignore your call, before he finally comes; you will just teach him to ignore your first four or five calls. Don't punish him when you get hold of him – you will teach him to be hard to catch. Just quietly bring him home. You can, in fact, click and treat the dog for letting you take hold of the collar; this defuses any tendency to stay out of reach.

When you are up against an extremely powerful distraction, such as the opportunity to play with another dog, you can use the distraction as a reinforcer. For example: take the dog to the park on a long leash and arrange to meet a friend with a dog. Let your dog look around and take note of his potential playmate. By and by, call your dog: if he comes, click and then, instead of giving a treat, unsnap the leash and let him go and play with his friend.

Then go and catch the dog, put the leash on, and go home. It seems counter-productive, I know, but each experience of this reinforcer will actually strengthen the behaviour of coming when called.

Sometimes, with a dog that has begun coming regularly and well, you arrive at a day when the dog suddenly seems totally deaf to your voice. You have reinforced coming when called many times, and now, suddenly, it doesn't seem to work. There is a negative move that you can make: Call the dog; give him an opportunity to succeed; and when he does not give the behaviour, take the dog straight home, without pausing for any more sniffs or fun. The next time you go out, you may see a return to his previous responsiveness. There is, of course, no point in doing this until the dog has already developed the behaviour of coming cheerfully when called.

 ## STEP FOUR: MAINTAINING COME

"Come" is such an important behaviour that I think it warrants attention throughout a dog's life. Use daily events to reinforce the "recall," the dog's quick return to you. For example: now and then, when you are going to give the dog his dinner, or a new toy or a chew bone, or when you are going to play with him, call the dog from wherever he is. When he comes, click, and then give him the dinner or the bone, or toss the ball or the Frisbee.

Most dogs love to ride in the car. If you are planning

"Come" must always mean good news. Here, a young Golden Retriever is being clicked for responding to "Come" as he gets into the car.

to take the dog somewhere in the car, use "Come," and reinforce the behaviour by opening the car door and letting the dog get in. As long as you own the dog, make "Come" very good news by following it, every once in a while, with a happy surprise. Some day, this practice may stand you in very good stead.

WALK ON A LOOSE LEASH

The technique we are engaging in is called "shaping." Instead of striving for one complete behaviour from the beginning, as we do in conventional training, we "build" the behaviour, bit by bit. There are many different ways to shape any given behaviour. Here are a number of ways to teach a dog to walk on a loose leash. If you have a confirmed puller already, you have some unto do, which will take a little longer. Experiment with these suggestions: train with your brain, not with your muscles.

STEP ONE

Take the puppy or dog to a quiet room or hall where you have enough room to walk around. Coax him to your left side, by patting your thigh and speaking his name. When he comes toward you, click. Give a treat.

Step forward with your left leg; coax the dog with a word or by patting your leg. *Don't* lure him with the treat – he will only learn to follow treats. You want him to learn to follow *you*. If he comes along with you, click and treat. Stop to treat, don't treat him "on the move;" it confuses the issue to have eating occurring simultaneously with the behaviour the dog is supposed to be learning. Where the dog is when he gets his treat should be irrelevant. What matters is that he is more or less beside your leg when you click.

Start up again; if the dog starts right up with you, click at once, stop and treat. Now take three steps before you click, and click if the dog is next to you. Turn around, coax the dog to come with you, and go back the other way. Click every three steps. If the dog is right with you, start clicking every four or five steps.

STEP TWO

Add variations. Go for longer numbers of steps. Try going a little faster, or a little slower. Make it easy for the dog to "win"; don't scold him if he moves away, just click him when he comes back.

Click the dog for staying close to your leg when you are turning, or reversing direction. Try stopping; click the dog for staying close when you stop. Go faster and slower. Keep those clicks coming every five to ten seconds, but be sure you have a reason for each click. Keep your sessions short – a few minutes is plenty.

 STEP THREE

Move outdoors. For safety's sake, put the dog on a leash; but tie the leash to your waist so you won't be tempted to yank the dog around, or to pull back if he pulls. (Most real plungers have actually been trained to pull forward by their owners constantly pulling back, while, nevertheless, letting the dog go wherever he wants.) Now go back to coaxing and clicking the dog every three steps, then every five, or ten, or whatever seems reasonable. Use your judgement; count how long the dog is staying with you as a rule, and make that your base line.

When the dog can go a long way, straight, without losing interest in you, start adding corners, curves and variations. Dogs love this game, and will begin to try to outguess you by staying close to your leg no matter *what* you think up to do. Make the game just hard enough to allow the dog lots of success.

What if the dog sees or smells something he wants to investigate, charges to the end of the leash, and starts pulling? Stop. Stand still. While the dog is pulling,

CLICKER TRAINING
WALKING ON A LOOSE LEASH

The handler has tied the leash around her waist so she cannot pull or yank Mich. She tries a few steps with Mich walking by her side on a loose leash.

Mich is clicked on the move, while she is offering the correct behaviour.

Stop walking to give the reward. You can make training more fun by throwing the treat for your dog to catch, but if the lead is attached to your waist, make sure you give an easy catch!

As your dog becomes proficient, you can make things more difficult by introducing distractions.

nothing happens. When the dog slackens, click. Treat.
Over many walks, you can increase the level of
temptation. Let the dog discover that, when he pulls,
nothing happens; but if the leash is slack, you will move
toward the other dog, the new person, the lamp-post, or
whatever he wants to investigate.

Your aim, with the clicker, is to give the *dog* the
responsibility for keeping the leash slack. By and by, it
will become a habit, and you will no longer have to
reinforce with praise or clicks more than once or twice
on a walk. And, eventually, you can expect good "leash
manners" as a matter of course.

A STEP FOR CONFIRMED PULLERS

The simple process of clicking every few steps, and
stopping to treat, repeated on a few different walks, is
often enough to convert inattentive pullers into
mannerly walking companions. Be sure to stop and let
the dog sniff and investigate, from time to time. That
pleasure should be permitted to the dog as a reward for
not pulling, instead of "stolen" by the dog's dragging
you to each thing he wants to smell.

What if the dog hits the trail pulling, and ignores you,
in the great outdoors? Tie the leash to your waist. If you
have a big dog, wear sturdy shoes so he can't pull you
off balance. Now you can use his desire to explore, as a
reinforcer. He pulls. You stop, plant your feet, and go
nowhere. Say nothing. When the dog looks at you, pat
your leg. If he slackens the leash or comes to you, click
and move forward. Immediately, he will probably plunge
to the end of the leash again, especially if he's been

THE CONFIRMED PULLER

A dog who wants to pull must learn that the 'correct' place to be is by your side. In this exercise, the handler is holding the leash, but it can also be trained with the leash tied around your waist.

Abi, a Japanese Spitz, may be small, but she is always keen to surge ahead.

She reaches the end of the leash, and has nowhere else to go.

The moment of decision – Abi is called back, and she is clicked as the lead goes slack.

As she returns to the handler's side, she is clicked again and given a reward.

doing that for years anyway. Repeat. Stop: slack leash, click and go.

You may not be able to go more than one step at a time, in the first session. That gets old in a hurry. Be prepared to quit early. When you get tired of this step-and-stop business, put the dog back indoors, or in the car. Try again the next day. Sooner or later the dog will capitulate, and he will start waiting for you instead of plunging ahead. *Then* you have something to click and treat.

AN EASY STEP

Sometimes you can cure a puller easily with one simple rule for yourself: Every time the leash goes slack, I will click and treat. Take the dog for a walk on the leash, in your usual fashion, but, again, tie the leash to your belt. When the dog, in his investigations, happens to let the leash go slack, click and treat. By the end of a ten-minute walk, you may have a reformed character.

Guess what? You can do this with two dogs. The rule is, "When *both* leashes are slack, I click and treat." Pay sharp attention; you may have a habit of letting the dogs pull that is so ingrained it's hard for you to notice those brief moments when they are not pulling. Did they stop to smell a bush, or scratch, or relieve themselves? It doesn't matter why. If one dog stopped, and then the other, click. Treat them both. Again, this can be an almost instant fix. Two or three five-minute walks, over two or three days, might be all that's needed, if your timing is right.

THE GENTLE LEADER

(1) *Griff is being introduced to the Gentle Leader. He is clicked as the handler puts it round his neck.*

(2) *The head collar is now being held in position, and Griff is rewarded for accepting the restraint.*

(3) *Click! The Gentle Leader is now ready to use.*

THE GENTLE LEADER

The Gentle Leader is a sort of halter for dogs, like a halter for horses. It goes around the nose and neck. The leash fastens under the jaw. The dog can still open his mouth comfortably; this is not a muzzle. However, if the dog pulls, his head is turned back or down so he can't see where he is going – so he stops pulling. You don't need to do any training at all. Just hold the leash and walk along. The dog may fight the collar at first, just as puppies fight a regular collar and leash at first; but he will soon teach himself to keep the leash loose. This is an excellent temporary fix while you are retraining the dog; or it can be a permanent help to a frail owner or a child who must walk a big dog.

CHAPTER THREE

IMPROVING YOUR SKILLS

Exercises to increase the complexity and to add variety

*C*licker training is a continuous process for both handler and dog, and one of the most stimulating aspects of this system of teaching is that you can keep adding to your dog's repertoire, improving his general behaviour, fine-tuning training exercises, or simply having fun and teaching tricks.

TARGET TRAINING

One of the most useful skills your clicker dog can learn is to touch a target, such as the end of a stick. One of the many uses of targeting is that you will be able to move the dog anywhere you like – off the couch, into the car, on to the grooming table, out from under the bed – without having to push, pull, or shove him, and with the dog's eager and interested co-operation.

 STEP ONE

Commercial folding aluminium target sticks are available on clicker training websites, but you can use anything: a dowel, a yard stick, or a two- to three-foot-long switch from an apple tree. For a tiny dog (or a cat) you might use a pencil or a chopstick.

Get your stick, treats, clicker, and dog. Rub a treat on the end of the stick, and allow your dog to sniff it. Click, and take the stick away from your dog's nose and give a treat. Repeat. Move the stick up an inch, down an inch, to the other side. Click for touching or even looking at the stick.

After a few clicks for touching, stand up and coax the dog to walk with you, holding the stick in front of him so

TARGET TRAINING

① *Rub a treat on the end of your target stick to encourage the dog to sniff it. Click as soon as the dog has touched the stick.*

② *Encourage the dog to follow the target, clicking every correct response.*

③ *Wysiwyg, a German Spitz, is now moving with confidence, following the target.*

① Chase, a Border Collie, is familiar with the target and is ready to follow it.

② The handler can direct him wherever she wants, using the target.

③ Chase can be taught to follow the target upwards or downwards. This can be very useful when training a dog for Agility.

he can touch it easily while he's walking. Somehow, dogs seem to catch on to targeting more quickly when they are moving. Click for each touch, stop, and treat, and continue. Lead him in left and right turns. See if you can get the dog to move around you in a quarter circle, then half a circle, then a full circle.

STEP TWO

When your dog is enthusiastic about his target stick, start using it for a few minutes now and then, during other activities: to lead the dog around obstacles (a wastebasket, for example), or under tables, through table legs, or over small jumps (a broomstick, or your extended leg.) Click and treat generously for the first successes; this is a great confidence-builder for timid dogs.

Take the dog outside and try targeting him over, and around, obstacles in this new and distracting environment. If he loses focus, go back to clicking and treating for just touching the stick from one inch away, or following it for just one to two steps of his paws. Use the target stick to get the dog into the car and out again, or into and out of a box or wheelbarrow. Use your imagination; every new success is good for the dog and builds his trust in you (and every success is a reward for you, too!)

STEP THREE

Try using other objects for targets: margarine tub lids are popular, because they are easy for the dog to see. Put

The target can also be used for training Sendaway – an exercise where the dog must leave his handler on command, and run out to a designated area. The target is fixed in place – but is clearly visible.

Griff is clicked for an enthusiastic response.

the lid on the floor and touch it with your target stick; click the dog for touching both. Or, hold the lid in your hand, click the dog for touching it, and gradually lower it to the floor and remove your hand. Put the lid in different parts of the room and click the dog for going away from you to touch it, wherever it is.

You can use both kinds of targets to teach your dog to negotiate agility obstacles. Extend the time the dog will stay on target. Just click him for holding his nose on the target for longer and longer periods, while you groom him, handle his feet, or clip his nails. The target can even be used when you are at the vet's to help the dog stay calm and hold still during medical examinations and treatment.

101 THINGS TO DO WITH A BOX

A Good Exercise For An Older, Suspicious, Or Previously Trained Dog

This game is derived from a dolphin research project by Karen Pryor and others. (See "The creative porpoise: training for novel behaviour," published in the *Journal of Experimental Analysis of Behaviour* in 1969.)

This training game has become a favourite with dog trainers. It is especially good for 'crossover' dogs with a long history of correction-based training, since it encourages mental and physical flexibility, and gives the dog courage to try something on his own.

 ## STEP ONE

Take an ordinary cardboard box (any size) cut the sides down to about three inches, and put the box on the floor. Click the dog for looking at the box. Treat. If the dog goes near or past the box, even by accident, click. Next, after you click, toss the treat near or in the box. If the dog steps toward the box to get the treat, click the step and toss another treat. If he steps into the box, great, click again, even if he is eating his previous treats, and offer him another treat in your hand.

Sometimes you can cook up a lot of "box action" in a hurry, this way: Click for stepping toward or in the box. Alternately toss the treat in the box and hold another treat out in your hand so the dog has to come back to you. If the dog is reluctant to step in the box, and so doesn't eat that treat, it doesn't matter: he knows he got it. If treats accumulate in the box, fine. When he does step into the box, he will get a jackpot. If you decide to stop the session before that happens, fine. Pick up the treats in the box, and put them away for a later session. Remember, never treat without clicking first, and always click for a reason: for some action of the dog's.

If you need more behaviour to click, you can move yourself to different parts of the room so the box is between you and the dog, increasing the likelihood of steps in the direction of the box. Don't call the dog, don't pat the box, don't chat, don't encourage the dog, don't "help" him. All of that stuff may just make him more suspicious. Click foot movements toward the box, never mind from how far away, and then treat. If you get in five or six good clicks, for moving in the direction or near or past the box, and then the dog "loses interest" and goes away, fine. You can always play "box" again later. In between sessions, the reinforcements you did get in will do their work for you; each little session will make things livelier the next time.

You are, after all, teaching your dog new rules to a new game. If you have already trained your dog by conventional methods, the dog may be respecting the general rule, "Wait to be told what to do."

The first rule of this new game, however, "Do something on your own, and I will click," is a toughie. In that case, the box game is especially valuable, and the first tiny steps are especially exciting – although they would be invisible to an onlooker, and may right now seem invisible to you.

101 THINGS TO DO WITH A BOX

Peg is a ten-year-old German Spitz. Here, she proves that you can teach old dogs new tricks. To start with, she is clicked for going near the box.

Do something on your own, and I will click it. This is a big step to take, so be patient while your dog works it out. In this case, Peg has placed her paw on the box.

When you bring the box out at your next training session, your dog will know that if he offers a behaviour, he will be clicked and a treat will follow. Peg is now showing great enthusiasm for the new game.

A leap on the box deserves a click...

...and so does a leap off!

Now Peg is trying something new – going inside the box. She will get clicked for this.

Encouraged by her success, Peg goes further in the box.

This exercise teaches dogs to be inventive. Peg knows she will only be clicked for offering a new behaviour, so now she tries a Down by the box. Click! That's a great way to end a training session.

End the first session with a "click for nothing" and a jackpot consisting of either a handful of treats, or a free grab at the whole bowl. Hmm. That'll get him thinking. The next time that cardboard box comes out, he will be alert to new possibilities. Clicks. Treats. Jackpots. "That cardboard box makes my person behave strangely, but on the whole, I like this new strangeness. Box? Something I can do, myself? With that box?" Those are new ideas, but they will come.

If your dog is very suspicious, you may need to do the first exercise over again once, or twice, or several times, until he "believes" something a human might phrase thus: "All that is going on here is that the click sound means my person gives me delicious food. And the box is not a trap, the box is a signal that click and treat-time is here – if I can just find out how to make my person click."

 STEP TWO

Whether these things occur in the same session or several sessions later, here are some behaviours to click. Click the dog for stepping in the box; for pushing the box, pawing the box, mouthing the box, smelling the box, dragging the box, picking up the box, thumping the box – in short, for anything the dog does with the box.

Remember to click *while* the behaviour is going on, not after the dog stops. As soon as you click, the dog will stop, of course, to get his treat. But because the click marked the behaviour, the dog will do that behaviour again, or some version of it, to try to get you to click again; so you do not lose the behaviour by interrupting it with a click.

You may end up in a wild flurry of box-related behaviour. *Great*! Your dog is already learning to problem-solve in a creative way. If you get swamped, and can't decide which thing to click, just jackpot and end the session. Now *you* have something to think about between sessions.

You may, on the other hand, get a more methodical, slow, careful testing by the dog: the dog carefully repeats just what was clicked before. One paw in the box, say. Fine: but right away *you* need to become flexible about what you click, or you will end up as a matched pair of behavioural bookends. Paw, click. Paw, click. Paw, click. That is not the way to win this game.

So, when the dog begins to offer the behaviour the same way, repeatedly, withhold your click. He puts the paw out, you wait. Your behaviour has changed; the dog's behaviour will change too. The dog might keep the paw there longer; fine, that's something new to click. He might pull it out; you could click that, once or twice. He might put the other paw in, too… fine, click that. Now he may try something new.

And? Where do we go from here? Well, once your dog has discovered that messing around with the box is apparently the point of this game, you will have enough behaviour to select from, so that you can now begin to click only for certain behaviours, behaviours which aim towards a plan. It's as if you had a whole box of Scrabble letters, and you are going to start selecting letters that spell a word. This process is part of "shaping".

 STEP THREE

Variations And Final Products: What Could You Shape From Cardboard Box Behaviours?

Get in the box and stay there. Initial behaviour: Dog puts paw in box. Click, toss treats. Then don't click, just wait and see. Maybe you will get two paws in box. Click. Now get four paws in box. Get dog in box. Options: Sitting or lying in box; staying in box until clicked; staying in box until called, then clicked for coming.

Uses: Put the dog to bed or in his crate. Let children amuse themselves and make friends with the dog by clicking the dog for hopping into a box and out again (works with cats, too). One third-grade teacher takes her Papillon to school in a picnic basket on special events days. When the basket is opened, the dog hops out, plays with the children, and then hops back in again.

BEHAVIOUR: Carry The Box

Initial behaviour: dog grabs the edge of the box in his teeth and lifts it off the floor.

Uses: Carry a box. Carry a basket. Put things away: magazines back on the pile. Toys in the toy box. A dog that has learned the generalised or generic rule, "Lifting things in my mouth is reinforceable," can learn many additional skills.

Behaviour: Tip The Box Over On To Yourself

I don't know what good this is, but it's not hard to get; it crops up often in the "101 things to do with a box" game. If the dog paws the near edge of the box hard enough, it will flip.

My Border Terrier, Skookum, discovered that he could tip the living-room wastebasket (wicker, bowl-shaped, empty) over on himself, so that he was hidden inside it. Then he scooted around in there, making the wastebasket move mysteriously across the floor. It was without a doubt the funniest thing any of our dinner guests had ever seen a dog do. Since terriers love being laughed with (but never *at*) clicks and treats were not necessary to maintain the behaviour once he had discovered it; and he learned to wait until he was invited to do it, usually when we had company.

INCREASING YOUR SKILLS

ADDING VARIATIONS

To keep the training interesting, and to make progress instead of getting stuck where you are, you need to keep adding to your requirements for clicking: you need to make the behaviour more complex, by asking the dog for more, before you click. For example, here are some ways you can increase the complexity of the simple "down."

Move away from the dog, and click him for staying down even though you have stepped back.

Move left, right, centre; jump up and down; do something noisy or silly; click the dog if he stays down

INCREASING THE COMPLEXITY

The Down is a straightforward exercise, but you can easily make it more difficult!

Rowan is clicked for staying in the Down while his handler moves to the side.

He is clicked for staying Down when the handler changes position.

Click! Rowan deserves a big reward for staying Down as his handler steps over him.

anyway. Walk around the dog; touch the dog and then step back again. Click him for staying "down." If he gets up, wait for him to "down" again. Then click for going down (and treat, of course). Then try your manoeuvre again, and give him another chance to experience staying down during your movements.

Play the "down" game in new places, such as outdoors. Don't be afraid to lure the dog down, once or twice. Then wait for him to go down, by himself, and click that. The first time you try clicking for "down" in new territory, you need to go "back to kindergarten" and make the task very easy for the dog.

Extend the length of time the dog has to lie down. Keep it varied: sometimes five seconds, sometimes twenty. Don't ask for more than thirty seconds from a little puppy. For a three-minute or five-minute down with no reinforcement, the dog needs to be old enough to tolerate boredom.

ESTABLISHING A CUE

Sometimes a dog who has learned one behaviour, such as "down," will start "throwing the behaviour at you" all day long: rushing up and crashing at your feet wherever you may be, in the hopes of getting a treat. This is the perfect time to teach the dog a signal, or cue: a name for the behaviour, such as the word, "Down."

You are going to show the dog, over a period of days, that lying down is still good for a click, but only after you have spoken the key word (or given the key signal) that means "down." You want the dog to discover, through repeated experiences, that going down on his own no longer leads to clicks and treats; but that he can be sure of getting a treat *if* he waits for the right cue before giving you a "down."

Say "Down," just before he is going to lie down anyway; click and treat. Coax him to get up. Repeat. After cueing him and reinforcing the down after the cue, two or three times, wait. Let him lie down. Do nothing. Coax him to get up. Say, "Down." Click the next down. Repeat this process, clicking for downs after the word, and ignoring downs that were not cued with the word. Repeat daily, eight or ten times, for a week. This is "respondent" conditioning. At first, it goes more slowly and takes more repetition than operant conditioning. Be patient; once the dog has learned two or three cues by repetition, with the cue gradually sinking in, he will be able to generalise: to understand the nature of a cue. Then subsequent cues will be learned more rapidly.

If you want to use a hand signal (many dogs respond better to hand signals than to words, at first) just replace the spoken cue in the instructions above with your chosen hand signal. A hand flung straight up in the air is the standard obedience cue for "Down."

When the dog is responding well to the signal, try signalling from further away, or when the dog is busy with other things, or in distracting circumstances. Your all-powerful clicker will be a great help in explaining to the dog that there is value in watching out for those cues or signals and responding to them any time, anywhere. (For more information about cueing behaviour, see Chapter 3, Stimulus Control, in Karen Pryor's book, *Don't Shoot the Dog*!)

TRAINING MULTIPLE BEHAVIOURS

You don't need to limit your clicker training to the programme outlined above. Right from the beginning, you can also leave clickers lying around the house and click the dog for other good behaviour, whenever it's convenient. For example, it's very helpful to click a puppy for relieving himself in the right place. House-training becomes infinitely easier with a clicker and treats by the door or in your coat pockets.

You can also click your puppy or older dog for other behaviour, such as standing still while you groom him. You will not confuse the dog by clicking for several behaviours. The clicker means "You win!" The dog will be delighted to learn that there are *many* ways to get his person to click. That will make the dog feel very smart!

FIND A TRAINING PARTNER

One good way to explore clicker training is to find a friend who also has a pet, and get started together. This chapter has given you several behaviours to try. If you and your friend each pick a different starting point, you will make discoveries you can share with each other; and you can reinforce each other for successes.

Team training is also very useful. Sometimes an observer can see what the dog is doing more easily than the handler, for example when training a dog to trot straight for the show ring, or to sit squarely for obedience work. One person can handle the dog and the treats, and ask for the behaviour. The other person watches, and clicks when the dog moves correctly. Then the handler treats.

GOING SOLO

For the most part, you can train on your own.
Here Toby, a Havanese, is being taught how to
wave.

Now he is being trained to
jump through his handler's
legs. This is the type of
movement that would be
used in a heelwork to
music routine.

You can take turns being the handler and the observer. You can handle your own dogs, or each other's. This way, the observer can concentrate entirely on studying the dog, and on clicking the with perfect timing, while the handler copes only with leash, food, and dog. Team

TEAMWORK

There are times when you need an assistant to operate the clicker. Here Toby is learning how to jump through his handler's arms.

training speeds up *your* learning, and gives the dog more accurate information. Besides, it's fun.

ADVANCE YOUR SKILLS
Use the resources available.
There is much more to operant conditioning than the basic shaping techniques outlined here. If you are developing a working dog, or a competition obedience dog, you should know about behaviour chaining, instructional reinforcers, stimulus transfer, and many other marvellous clicker-training tools. See Resources (pages 111) for suggestions about books and videos that you may find interesting as you gain more skills.

CHAPTER FOUR

CLICKER TIPS

*Easy-to-follow advice for
new clicker trainers*

If you are working with the "Getting Started" section, these tips will serve as a review. They cover many of the common mistakes novice clicker trainers make.

Always Click First, Then Treat

In this kind of training, you do not need to keep the food in front of the dog, to bait or lure the dog. What your pet is doing *when the treat arrives* is not important. Your pet will remember what he was doing *when he heard* the click. After you click, you can let the behaviour stop, give the treat, and then go back to the training, without causing problems.

Always Click While The Behaviour Is Happening

The "click" is like an acoustic arrow; it goes right into the animal's nervous system with the message, "What your body is doing at this instant has just paid off." Use it at the moment that counts. If you are teaching your dog to jump, for example, don't click before the dog goes over the jump. Don't click after the dog has completed the jump. Don't click when you think he is going to jump. Click when the dog is in the air. Once the dog is jumping, you can improve the way the dog lands, for example, by clicking at the moment of landing correctly. The food can come later; the click carries the message.

Only Click Once

Resist the temptation to make multiple clicks – clickety clickety clickety – for especially good behaviour. The

GETTING THE TIMING RIGHT

Chase is being trained to stand in a show pose. He is clicked for the pose, and he knows a treat will follow.

Catch it! Chase is rewarded with a treat.

timing of the click is crucial; it is when you click that tells the animal exactly what you liked. If you click over and over, the animal can't tell which click is the meaningful one, and the behaviour will not improve. Furthermore, your pet might decide only multiple clicks are worth working for.

Don't Use Your Clicker To Get The Dog's Attention, Or To Get The Dog To Come

Sure, it will work that way, at first, anyhow. If you have had trouble with those things in the past, that new response may be reinforcing for you, so you are tempted to try it over and over again. Watch out, though!

If you continue to call your dog with the clicker, or to click to try to distract the dog from other interesting things, you will lose the clicker's power as information for the dog.

Don't Use Your Clicker For Encouragement, Or As A Start Signal

You should always be thinking, "What am I actually reinforcing?"

If your dog hesitates, or lags behind you, and you click to encourage him, you are reinforcing hesitation or lagging. Click only for behaviour you want.

Use The Right Size And Type Of Food Treat

Here are some common-sense rules about food treats:

- Start your training when the pet is hungry. Many dog owners do a five-minute clicker training session before the dog's breakfast or dinner.
- Don't leave food down all day long; feed your pet at specific times. If you need to leave food available most of the time (as vets recommend for most birds and small animals), take the food away for two or three hours just before your training session.
- Make your treats part of the pet's total food intake; if you are using a lot of treats, cut back on the pet's normal food a little.
- Find out what your dog really loves to eat for his treat.
- Keep the training fun. Always toss in a few easy tasks when you are working on hard ones.

Vary The Difficulty Of The Task

I hated my piano lessons, as a child. Whenever I mastered a piece, instead of getting to have fun playing it, I just got a newer, harder piece to struggle over.

Don't make your sessions go from old, easy stuff to new, hard stuff every time – that's a great way to teach your pet to hate training and want to quit early. Particularly when you are extending the duration of a behaviour, go back and forth between easier and harder.

Are you teaching the dog to stay on his mat for 30 seconds? Click for 10 seconds, then 25, 15, 35, 10, 40, and so on.

Keep the dog hopeful of success. Always end the session with something easy and fun, where the animal can be sure of earning reinforcement.

Keep Your Training Sessions Short And Varied
Don't practise the same thing over and over again
Train in short bursts. Three sessions, each five minutes long, will do you more good than three half-hour sessions in which you and the pet both get tired. You do not need to drill or practise this kind of training to make it "sink in."

Experienced correction-style trainers are often amazed to find that behaviour trained by shaping and reinforcement does not deteriorate. With your clicker you can communicate to your pet. The pet will remember whatever you have communicated successfully, and will eagerly offer to do it again, even if days, weeks, or months have passed between sessions.

PROGRESSING IN SMALL STEPS

The Italian Greyhound is not a natural retriever, but, by building up the exercise in small stages, and clicking for each correct behaviour, Whilan soon got the idea.

1. Here, Whilan is being shown his toy, and is being encouraged to play with it.

2. To begin with, he is hesitant as he approaches the toy. He is clicked for showing interest.

3. The click for showing interest has boosted his confidence, and he is now becoming quite playful. He will be clicked for this.

4. A big step forward, Whilan is ready to pick up the toy. Click!

5. It is now time to put the exercise together. The handler prepares to throw the toy.

6. Whilan runs out and picks up the toy. Initially he will be clicked for this. As he becomes more proficient, he will not need to be clicked for each stage, he will string the whole exercise together, and be clicked and rewarded on completion.

7. Whilan returns to his handler.

8. Click! Whilan brings the toy back to his handler. Now he is given a treat.

Expect To Progress In Small Steps

In generic or traditional training, we ask for the whole behaviour from the first ("Heel!" meaning "Walk right next to me wherever I go") and correct any departure from that behaviour, until the animal can do the behaviour for prolonged periods without needing "correction." Shaping behaviour with reinforcement is different. We build behaviour in little steps. The animal discovers how to earn reinforcers at each new step. It takes more brains and thought from the trainer but the rate of progress can be spectacular.

Nevertheless, sometimes the learning "hits a plateau," where the dog doesn't seem to make any improvement for quite a while. Hang in there: a plateau often precedes a huge leap forward. It helps to start each training session with a little review.

If A Behaviour Your Dog Knows Well Suddenly Falls Apart, "Go Back To Kindergarten"

Sometimes a change in circumstances makes more difference to an animal than we might think. For example, a dog that heels beautifully, or comes when called perfectly, in your house, or yard, or at the training school, may act as if he has never heard those words before in a new place. Don't scold! Instead, pretend you never trained the behaviour, and go back to the first thing you ever clicked for, even if it was "Come from three feet away for a click and a treat." Then proceed up through the increasing difficulty of the task, just the way you first shaped it, but in the new circumstances. (You can keep a leash on the dog while you do this, for safety's sake.)

We call this "Going back to kindergarten". This quick review of the shaping procedure is sometimes all you need to establish the behaviour in a new environment. It may take one session, or several, but it will certainly go much faster than it did the first time. Be sure to give a jackpot of great treats if it works in one training session!

Don't Think You Can Read The Dog's Mind

His feelings, yes: we can sometimes tell from a dog's attitude how he feels about things (sometimes we're wrong, too). But why he feels some way, or why he is doing something, is guesswork at best.

When the dog does not do what you expected, you can always find people who will insist it happened *because* of some reason. The dog is "stressed." The dog is "ring-wise." The dog is "trying to get back at you." The dog is "too dominant." The dog "must have been abused," etc. Then they tell you how to *fix* their imagined cause, often by punishment.

Don't listen! If a behaviour your pet knows well suddenly falls apart, don't spend a lot of time wondering why. You may never know the reason. Maybe the dog thought the rules only worked if you were wearing white shoes, and you are now wearing your new purple Adidas. Just go back to kindergarten, review the shaping, and reinforce easier steps, until the behaviour reappears.

Quit While You're Ahead

It's always tempting, when we get a wonderful behaviour, to try to make it happen again and again, until the subject makes a mistake and the behaviour breaks down. Learn to quit when you get something good. Leave a success in the dog's mind. If you are not making progress, and you want to stop training, go to something easy that you know you can click the dog for before you stop training.

Have Fun!

If you find yourself getting frustrated or angry, stop right there. You cannot do this kind of training when you are angry. Wait and try again later. Trainer Catherine Crawmer says the most important tool in reinforcement training is a cup of tea! When you feel baffled, sit down and have some tea, and think. Don't display your anger to the dog: it teaches the dog nothing except that you are unpredictable.

CHAPTER FIVE

BUT WHAT ABOUT...?

Frequently asked questions

"Help! I Don't Know Where To Begin."

Don't begin by trying to fix some problem. The clicker is for starting behaviour, not for stopping it. One easy way to start is to "go fishing" for a new behaviour. If your dog already knows the behaviours described in Chapter 2, pick some simple trick, like turning in a circle, bowing, shaking hands, or touching a target, and use that as your first practice behaviour.

"My Dog Is Afraid Of The Clicker. I Clicked At Him And He Ran And Hid Under The Bed."

The dog is afraid of the clicker because he does not know what it means. He lacks the correct information. That may make him suspicious (some dogs, not unwisely, associate any new experience with going to the veterinarian).

If you have a suspicious dog, you can click as you drop treats into his food bowl.

Don't worry about the fear; work on giving him the information. You can soften the sound a bit by clicking the clicker in your pocket, or behind your back. You can really muffle the clicker by putting several layers of adhesive tape over the "dimple" in the metal part. Now click – just once – as you put his dinner down; or just as you start to toss him a special treat or give him a special toy. Click (just once, in your pocket) when you let the dog out (or back in) or start out the door on your walk together.

Find an excuse to use the clicker to say "Something nice is coming" at several intervals during the day and evening. How many click-events do you think it will take, across three days, for your dog to decide a click is pretty good news?

"What If My Dog Doesn't Like Treats, And Won't Work For Food?"

At a trainers' picnic, a dog owner told me his German Shepherd was a picky eater and wouldn't work for food – while behind his back the dog was stealing fried chicken scraps from discarded paper plates. I cut up some chicken and clicker trained the dog to follow a target stick in about five minutes. Moral: to start with, use a preferred food.

It's true that some dogs are legitimately suspicious, or even cynical, about treats: free food in the past may have had bad consequences from the dog's point of view. So, if you have a dog like that, go slow. Just click and treat, click and treat, a few times, twice a day, for no particular behaviour, at no particular time.

You could stand by the dog's bowl and toss the treats in, after each click. Even if the dog is very suspicious, he will hear the food fall in. Once the dog decides you have no nefarious plans up your sleeve, he will eat the food. Once he learns a few ways to make you click and treat, the dog will start to love the treat more! Try it and see.

"What If We Have More Than One Dog?"

Separate the dogs – work with one at a time and put the others outside, or in the laundry room, or in their crates, or in the kitchen. Sure, the others will hear the clicks; they will not get the treats, so they will not be confused – just eager for their turn.

"How Long Should A Training Session Be? How Often Should I Train?"

Five-minute sessions, whenever you can fit them in, are the best way to start. Scientists have proved that dogs, pets, and people learn more in several short sessions than they do in one long session. Short sessions are more fun and less tiring, and easier to fit into a busy schedule, too.

"Can I Train More Than One Behaviour In A Single Session?"

Yes, of course. You can work on come, and sit, and then heel, and throw in a trick or two in any one session. Changing around is fun. What you should *not* do, however, is work on more than one detail of any given behaviour in a single reinforcement. If, for instance, you are working on "Trotting with your tail held high" (a

CHOOSING A REWARD

Some dogs will work better if a toy is offered as the reward.

Wysiwyg is being trained to Stay at a distance from her handler. She is clicked for offering the correct behaviour.

Her reward is running out to retrieve her ball.

nice behaviour for the show ring), just click or withhold clicks for that; don't suddenly scold the dog for lagging behind. "Not lagging" is a different task. Work on it separately.

"I Teach Dog Classes, With A Lot Of Dogs And People In One Room. I Can't See How We Could Use Clickers, With Ten People Clicking All Over The Place."
Actually, you *can* use clickers in classes; many modern trainers do. Most dogs hear better than we do. They

GROUP TRAINING

Clicker training works in group sessions. These three dogs are showing excellent attention, despite their close proximity to each other.

A new set of dogs and a big test of concentration. The handlers turn their backs, and the dogs must stay in position until the handlers return.

know where their owners are, who has their treats, and where the sound is coming from. Even a dog can figure out "That's *my* click" in about three clicks.

A verbal "click", a word, is not as unique and distinct as the clicker, so it is not as useful for learning new skills and behaviour, but it will serve to keep already-learned behaviour going. Some people also use a special touch – a light tap on the dog's head or back, for instance – as a substitute for the click: very handy in the show ring.

"What Happens If I Make A Mistake In Training? Will I Ruin The dog?"

If you make a mistake, laugh and pet your dog. It is easy to click too soon or too late, or for the wrong thing, or to miss a great chance for reinforcement, and we all do it all the time. In the long run, you will get enough clicks in at the right times to communicate to your dog what it is that you want. While an erroneous punishment can do all kinds of damage to the learning process, an erroneous reinforcement or two is harmless. Clicker-training is creative, interactive, and cumulative; it is a very forgiving system.

"What Do I Do If A Dog Makes A Mistake?"

Don't click. That's all. Don't say "No," or jerk the leash, or push the dog in the right direction. Adding punishment, correction, or coercion to this system does not help the dog understand how to earn clicks. It does not make the dog more reliable, despite the widespread conviction of many trainers that force is necessary. It definitely does make the dog less interested in learning.

"But Doesn't That Mean I Should Never Punish The Dog? What If The Dog Jumps Up, Or Nips Me, Or Takes Food Off The Counter, Or Runs Away?"

Some people think that using positive reinforcement means you never reprimand the dog or control him physically. That's unrealistic. Leashes are a fact of life for dogs. It's necessary to keep a dog on a leash when you are going to strange places, or out in traffic, or among strange dogs. And, of course, your dog needs to understand the meaning of "No."

You need to interrupt behaviour such as mouthing your hands and clothes, for example, or chewing the furniture. Remember that timing is just as important in correcting misbehaviour as it is in reinforcing good behaviour. Your response should occur while the behaviour is happening, not afterwards, or just before you think it might happen.

While correction and scolding can stop behaviour (while you're around, anyway), they are not efficient ways to teach the dog to do something new. For that, clicks and treats work best. As for stealing food, tipping over the garbage, and so on, it's up to you to monitor the environment and put temptation out of reach.

"Isn't It Necessary To Make The Dog Respect Me, Even Fear Me, If I Want Long-Term Reliability?"
You will find that the more things your dog learns *to do*, the more he will trust and respect you, and the easier it will become to make him understand what he should *not do*.

Furthermore, training with reinforcement creates a dog that is doing things because he *wants* to do them. He understands what the job is, and he is confident of a successful outcome. That's true reliability.

"You Don't Say Much About Commands; When Do I Tell The Dog What To Do?"
When the dog has learned the behaviour. First the dog learns that sitting is good for a click and treat. Then the dog learns that sitting only gets a click and a treat when

VARY THE ROUTINE

*Make sure training sessions are enjoyable for both
you and your dog. In between training exercises,
you can have fun teaching a new trick. Here,
Mich shows off her 'gangster' routine.*

① *Hands up!*

② *Shooting from the hip...*

③ *Roll over and play dead!*

The clicker can take the guessing out of Obedience work.

you say "Sit!" So the word becomes a signal that treats are now available for that particular action.

When we are training with punishment – with leash corrections, for example – it is only fair to warn the dog first. Thus we say "Heel", before we pull the dog along with us, right from the beginning. What this command means from the dog's point of view is: "Heel or *else* you will be jerked." The dog learns to do the right behaviour to avoid getting pushed or pulled.

With clicker training, there is no point in making meaningless sounds at the dog, until the dog has learned the behaviour. The command, in traditional training, is a warning signal. The cue, as the signal is often called in reinforcement training, is a green light for a particular action that has paid off many times in the past.

"What If I Give The Cue And The Dog Doesn't Do It?"

Then you have not established the cue under that circumstance. Here's a common event: a dog may "come" when called beautifully at home, but in a park with squirrels he's suddenly deaf. It doesn't mean he's disobedient, it just means the trainer has not yet asked for and reinforced "Come" often enough under these new conditions.

One might have to train (on leash, at first, and step by step) "Come in strange places", "Come from afar", and "Come, even when there are squirrels". You can get there, faster and more surely, by shaping the behaviour step by step, than by getting mad, or punishing a failure to respond.

Clicker training is a great asset in Agility training, as the dog can be reinforced by the clicker at a distance. Photo: Karen Pryor.

"When Can I Cut Out The Food?"

That's a popular question. The click, and the treat, are for learning a new behaviour, or for learning to do it in new or tougher circumstances. Once the behaviour is learned, you will not need to treat for that behaviour any longer, as a regular thing.

"What If I Want To Go Into Obedience Training, Or Some Other Form Of Competition, With My Dog?"

The clicker is a superb tool for explaining to the obedience dog just what the nature of the task is, from perfect heeling to advanced exercises such as scent discrimination. Brainy trainers everywhere are pioneering in developing ways of shaping traditional exercises with reinforcement instead of with correction.

New books and videos are in development. More and more trainers are using reinforcement training to develop everything from household pets to police patrol dogs; but everywhere in dogdom it is still a rather new idea.

Jump in! The rest of the pioneers need your input!

"How Can You Use Clicker Training For Obedience, When Everyone Knows You Can't Use A Clicker Or Treats In The Obedience Ring?"

Once again, the clicker and treats are a tool for learning the behaviour. Once you get into the show ring, the learning part should be already accomplished. By now, you have substituted a verbal cue for the click, and petting and praise for the treat; so you don't need them in the show ring.

The dogs that "fall apart" in the ring are often dogs that have been trained by correction. As they spend more and more time in competition, they make more and more mistakes in the ring; not because they "know" they won't get corrected, but because the absence of correction conveys the information that what the dog is doing is what he is supposed to do.

Ironically, you are allowed to praise your dog in the obedience ring, but you are not allowed to correct him. So training with reinforcers actually gives you an advantage in communicating with your dog in the ring.

"My Dog Has Already Had A Lot Of Obedience Training. How Do I Mix Clicker Training Into What He Already Knows?"

Don't start by working on behaviour your dog already knows. Start with tricks or something new. Morgan Spector, an obedience teacher and competitor who has changed from traditional methods to clicker training, calls this a "crossover dog."

Crossover dogs (and crossover trainers) have a lot to unlearn as well as a lot to learn. It can be harder, in some ways, for experienced traditional trainers to learn clicker training than for rank beginners.

CHAPTER SIX

THE CLICKER REVOLUTION

*Looking at the
wider applications*

DOGS AND PEOPLE LEARNING TOGETHER

While the science underlying clicker training has been around since the 1940s, and the principles were in use among marine mammal trainers beginning in about 1960, it wasn't until the 1990s that this new technology really began spreading to pet owners. Perhaps my book, *Don't Shoot the Dog!,* the first popular text on operant conditioning, prepared the ground; but I think the change really began when dog owners, not just dog trainers, got that little clicker in their hands and began discovering what they could do with it.

Instead of noticing all the bad things their dogs were doing, people found themselves watching for something that they liked: something to click. The click not only rewarded the dog, it changed the owner's attitude. Instead of trying to 'fix' the dog, and stop the problems, owners began looking for good behaviour, and rewarding that; and the problems usually went away by themselves. People discovered that their dogs were smarter than they thought, and lots more fun.

The attitudes of the dogs changed, too. This person with a clicker, who perhaps used to be largely an impediment to whatever the dog wished to do, now became an exciting and valuable acquaintance. A dog that had discovered ways to make the owner click became much more focused on the owner, and much more interested in what the owner wanted. Two beings that often had been at odds with each other now became partners, learning together. Clicker magic! And all it took was a few clicks. No wonder people were converted.

CHANGING ATTITUDES

Dogs and their owners get tuned into each other with clicker training. Rowan has learnt to bring the mail. It is a useful task, and he enjoys the opportunity to be successful.

Furthermore, training with a clicker didn't require physical skills or years of practice. It was easy to learn. You could pick up the basics from a book like this one, or a video, or on the Internet. As in learning to use email, to do word processing, or to surf the Web, you could get started without a teacher. You could develop skills in brief sessions around the house. You could easily pass on the basics to other people who asked, "How did you do that? Show me!" Seminars, classes, and teaching programmes helped to spread the word and develop the technology. The Internet became a huge source of information and support, through websites, chat groups, and, above all, email listservs, starting with the original Clicker List.

As people discovered how to clicker train, and helped each other to learn more, clicker clubs and centres sprang up all over the world, from Finland to Tasmania, Singapore to Sweden, Russia to Brazil. Wonderful and innovative techniques and applications blossomed independently, in Germany, in the UK, in Australia, and across the US, as one new clicker trainer after another developed his or her own clicker solutions, and then wrote about them, or made a video, or started teaching in person or on the Internet. By 2002, at least 300,000 people were clicker training according to Internet data. This movement, while based in science, was created of and by people themselves – and their wonderful pets.

CLICKING SPREADS

At Sea Life Park in Hawaii, where I began working with this technology in 1963, we dolphin trainers developed a vast variety of behaviours. These were trained with a marker signal, reinforcers, and verbal or gestural cues, in many animals, including wild free-flying sea birds, seals, dogs, feral Hawaiian pigs, jungle fowl, fish and octopi – and, of course, our own pets at home. We knew that clicking worked for any living being. But, in spite of the increasingly widespread use of clicker training with dogs, it was not immediately obvious to conventional trainers that the clicker could be useful for other animals, too.

Alexandra Kurland, a horse trainer and dressage rider, sparked the first breakthrough with her 1998 book, *Clicker Training for Your Horse*. Soon thousands of people in the United States, Canada, United

The clicker has become a powerful tool in the horse world.

Kingdom, and in Europe, especially in Germany, were experimenting with this remarkable new way to teach horses everything they need to know – without spurs, bits, whips, and force. Newly-converted riders and trainers were producing articles, books, videos, and new applications. The horses appreciated it, learned fast, and worked much more willingly. Clicker training became a powerful way to put the finishing touches on a highly-trained competition horse; to rehabilitate an aggressive or dangerous horse; to train foals and yearlings; and to make any horse safe and manageable. Thousands of amateurs, with no conventional horse training background, discovered that they could use clicker training to turn their own horse, perhaps once resistant and troublesome, into a co-operative, intelligent partner and friend.

Cats adapt surprisingly well to clicker training. Photo: Karen Pryor.

Of course, clicker training works for other kinds of pets and domestic animals, too. Clicker training owners have taught dog agility routines to goats and donkeys. Clicker training is the standard method for owners and breeders of llamas and alpacas, animals popular in the western United States as pets and pack animals and for their wool. Books, videos, websites, and listservs are devoted to clicker training for cats. Clicker training for cute behaviours is a delightful way to interact, amuse and exercise an indoor cat, and to replace undesirable behaviour with entertaining and healthy activity.

Birds, especially parrots and their relatives, have become enormously popular pets as breeding in captivity makes them more available. The parrot family

can be troublesome to manage, though, given to
screaming, biting, and pulling out their feathers; and
punishment just makes things much worse. Clicker
training to the rescue: using positive reinforcement with
a marker signal, even a beginner can soon get on better
terms with these bright and interesting – but highly
emotional – pets. Bird clicker trainers have also
established websites and listservs to help each other out.

The smaller mammals, such as mice, gerbils, rats, and
rabbits, make great clicker pals, especially for children of
nine years or older. Clicker training a small pet makes a
fine science project for school, and it provides
something interesting to do with the pet besides feeding
it and cleaning the cage. Many rodents will accept treats
and store them in their nest, making it easy to click lots
of behaviour. Small pets can be trained to do gymnastics
and run obstacle courses, to follow a target such as a
pencil or a laser pointer, to carry small objects and put
them in bottles or boxes, and to jump or run through
hoops and tunnels on cue. And why draw the line at
mammals? One can easily train a fish – as long as it is
healthy and eating vigorously – to swim through a hoop
or jump to a target, using favourite foods as the treat
and a flashlight blink as the click.

WORKING DOGS

Clicker training is easy and fun for pet owners, and has
made life better for many a household dog. But could it
ever replace traditional, time-honoured methods for
training working dogs, such as service/assistance dogs
that help the handicapped; police dogs that track

Police handlers have found the clicker is particularly helpful when training 'sniffer dogs' to detect drugs and explosives.

criminals and help to capture them; and dogs that find hidden drugs and explosives?

Well, yes, if the trainer is willing to experiment. Steve White, a police officer in Seattle, Washington, pioneered the development of clicker training for police work, including tracking and protection, and has taught his techniques to many other trainers in law enforcement. Officer White also teaches clicker training for the search dogs that locate hidden or illegal substances such as drugs, explosives, money, or contraband foodstuffs.

Positive reinforcement, using a marker signal of some sort to provide the dog with accurate information, can facilitate the training of sniffer dogs, whatever they are searching for. Experiments are underway in several countries using operant conditioning for dogs trained to locate landmines. One potential advantage is that clicker training can be taught to local handlers, and mine-sniffing skills can be learned by local dogs. At present, however, the methods of organisations that provide dogs for these and other search tasks range from completely traditional to completely modern, with most falling somewhere in between.

While the training of guide dogs for the blind remains, as a rule, fairly traditional, programmes are more likely to be positively based in the relatively new field of training "service" dogs for the handicapped. These dogs can carry baskets and other objects, pick up things that have been dropped, find and retrieve mobile phones, the TV remote, and other objects, turn lights and appliances on and off, close and open doors, provide steadying support for walking or standing, and pull wheelchairs.

Many of these programmes, such as Dogs for the Disabled in Great Britain, rely on positive reinforcement rather than conventional correction-based training. Nina Bonderenko, director of Canine Partners for Independence, also in Great Britain, develops service dogs entirely by clicker training. Volunteers clicker train puppies from eight weeks on, for house-training and general good manners. Formal training of service dog skills is also shaped with the clicker.

Recipients of the trained dogs learn clicker training too, so that they can go on adding to the dog's repertoire on their own. Just as important, a person with a physical disability usually finds it much easier to

WORKING PARTNERS

Assistance dog Endal, trained by Canine Partners For Independence, shows the high standard of work that can be achieved using the clicker. Photos: Veronica Morgan, CPI.

maintain the dog's behavioural skills by clicking for the right behaviour than by the more traditional system of physically correcting erroneous behaviour.

HOW ABOUT PEOPLE?

Of course, positive reinforcement works with people, and a marker signal is much more accurate than a spoken word in catching behaviour as it happens, even in human beings. However, I suppose one might feel a little conspicuous clicking a child for behaving nicely on the bus, say, or in a restaurant. In fact, it's the thought that counts; once you get used to thinking the clicker way, you are much more likely to notice good behaviour and reward it, instead of giving your attention to a child only when it's doing something wrong.

Where clicker training actually works brilliantly in humans is in the teaching of physical skills involving timing. Gymnastics is a sport in which things happen much faster than a coach can speak; but a click for correct movement reaches the gymnast even in mid-air. People are experimenting with clickers in training singers, in language training, and in teaching complex multi-part tasks such as flying a plane. And retention of skills learned in this way is permanent. For example, a friend of mine used the clicker to teach his three-year-old daughter to balance on ice skates; six months later, when skating season came around again, she balanced perfectly from the start.

The laws of learning are scientific laws; that's what makes clicker training work. The *technology* of clicker training, however – the rules we are discovering for

Most important of all – clicker training is fun for both dogs and trainers.

ourselves as we clicker train – are not yet fully understood. Does the clicker get faster results than a spoken word? Yes, we know that empirically, from all the reports by people who have taught classes with words as the marker signal, and then taught the same material using the clicker. They find that both dogs and their owners learn the new behaviours in half the time, with clicks; we can say it happens, but we certainly can't yet say why.

Then there are the side-effects of clicker training, such as the visible excitement and elation in the learner, and possible changes in brain activity and blood chemistry. Many young scientists, especially a group of students at the University of North Texas, are researching these and other questions raised by clicker training; some day we will have answers that we don't have now.

What we do now have are the observations of thousands of people who have become clicker trainers – and who have noticed and reported results, not just in the learners they are training, but in themselves. Here's what people seem to be finding:

Whether you are working with a pet, a person, or a corporation, the concepts that make up the tools in the clicker trainer's kit lead you to respond in new ways. You become used to the idea that behaviour needs to be built in small pieces, not in big chunks. You stop expecting too much, too soon, and just look for what you can reinforce – and so, in fact, you get more results, and faster.

If you see a behaviour you don't like, being a clicker trainer, instead of rushing in to prevent it or stop it, you take it as a training opportunity: what is it this learner needs to know? What's missing? What can I add that would replace this bad behaviour? You don't try to push people around with threats and anger, if that was once your style, or with nagging and complaint; you have a better way – reinforcing what you like, instead of attacking what you don't. Some people talk about 'internalising' the clicker training. Other people just say that once you've crossed over, you can't go back. Again, there are lots of unanswered questions; but any clicker trainer will tell you that this new technology is more than just a training short-cut. The experience can lead to less stress and more fun in life – for you, for your pets, and maybe for everyone else around you, too. Click!

CLICKER RESOURCES

GETTING STARTED
Visit the website *www.clickertraining.co.uk* and you'll find plenty of information and news on all aspects of clicker training. You can also buy a full range of clicker products direct.

Clickers: The highest quality clickers, as used by Karen Pryor. Available in packs of four.
Price: £4.99

FOR CATS

Clicker Training For Cats
Yes, you can train that cat. The revolutionary new clicker training method will yield results that will amaze you – and your cat. Published May 2002.
Price: £7.99

FOR HORSES

Clicker Training For Your Horse
In this remarkable book, Alexandra Kurland shows how to use the techniques of positive reinforcement and shaping with a horse. You'll find that you and your "clicker horse" develop the kind of mutual trust and friendship most owners only dream of having.
Price £25

Order direct via
Ringpress Books
Phone: 01594 845577
Fax: 01594 845599
e-mail: orders@ringpress.co.uk

**'Clicker
Training and
Friskies
Winalot – a
rewarding
combination'**
– Karen Pryor